Dedicated to anyone who has ever left their home country voluntarily or out of necessity. There are no borders on freedom, opportunity, safety, and hope.

This is Lucy.

Lucy has a big heart, lopsided ears, and a story to tell.

Lucy was born in Central America—Panama, to be exact—near the equator where it is warm all year round.

The people of Panama are also warm and very friendly. The family Lucy belonged to had not planned on having a dog and did not have enough money to take care of her properly.

They worked hard all day, so they could not be around to take her for walks and teach her how to be a good dog.

When they weren't home, Lucy would roam around her little town looking for food scraps and would try to avoid the mean neighborhood dogs.

But they would follow her around and when she would find something really good to eat, they'd try to take it. She would have no choice but to defend the food she'd worked so hard to find.

Uncertainty, hunger, and fighting were a regular part of Lucy's life. Then, one day, Lucy heard about a place where dogs were given two meals a day, slept indoors on cozy beds, and had all the belly rubs they could ever want.

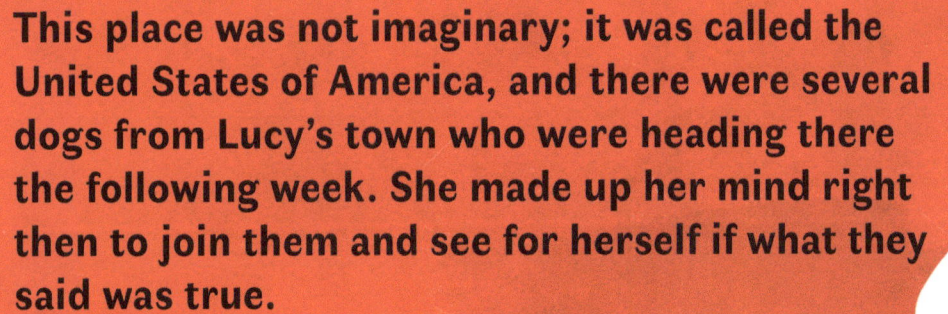

This place was not imaginary; it was called the United States of America, and there were several dogs from Lucy's town who were heading there the following week. She made up her mind right then to join them and see for herself if what they said was true.

The trip was long and they added to their caravan of hopeful dogs as they travelled. Sometimes, it was beautiful and serene, like in Costa Rica, where monkeys swing from the lush jungle trees.

Other times, it was dangerous, like in Mexico's Chihuahuan Desert, where the days are very hot and there isn't enough water.

But they were determined to make it and experience a happier and safer life.

After a month of walking, they successfully arrived in San Diego, California. They were excited and ready to find the loving homes they'd heard about. Lucy said goodbye to her travel companions and found a nice park to sleep in for the night.

That night, she had optimistic dreams of her new family and home. The next morning, she woke up bright and early and set off to make her dream a reality.

There was a coffee shop next to the park where people were having breakfast outside. Lucy saw a couple she thought looked nice and approached them. She pressed up softly against the man's leg and placed little kisses on the woman's knees. The couple immediately fell in love with Lucy's wide smile and silly ears. They noticed she had no collar or identifying tags, but they'd heard about dogs coming across the border for help.

The couple was finishing up a road trip and were heading home to Colorado the next day. Obviously, they hadn't planned on taking a dog back home with them but they couldn't imagine leaving Lucy alone to take care of herself. So, with big ideas and the best intentions, they made room in their car and a place in their family for Lucy.

Lucy was street smart and knew her fate had turned when she was adopted by the nice couple from America. But she couldn't have prepared herself for what she was about to experience.

First, there was the was vast size of the landscape. Homes and businesses were far apart. In Panama, Lucy knew where her family worked and would sometimes visit them during the day. But now, she didn't know where her new family went. Her surroundings made her feel very small.

Then, there were the fenced yards. They were very nice, with soft green grass and lots of shade. But Lucy had never been confined like this before. She was used to being free to wander whenever and wherever she wanted.

Lastly, there was the language barrier. In Panama, the language spoken is Spanish but in the United States, people speak English. Lucy learned basic words like "sit" and "good girl" but when she was out in the neighborhood, she was often confused and overwhelmed.

She was safer and healthier than she'd ever been but Lucy felt very foreign and alone. On most days, she would just sleep or hide so she didn't have to go outside and be reminded of how little she understood about her new surroundings.

The neighborhood dogs didn't make things any easier. They didn't understand her barking or her unusual manners. When they chased a squirrel or a frog, they did it for fun. But because of her past,

Lucy knew how to actually catch smaller animals, which seemed weird to the other dogs. They made fun of her differences and didn't include her in their play.

When Lucy ventured out for a walk, she would often revert to her old defensive behavior as a way of coping with her sadness. She felt bad about herself when she didn't understand what another dog wanted, so she would start a fight to get out of the situation. It didn't take long for word to spread that Lucy—the new dog—spoke oddly, acted funny, and was mean. So, all the other dogs started to avoid her.

Lucy became difficult and refused to learn any more English. She was grumpy and distant with her affection and was not at all the dog the couple had fallen in love with. Then, one day in October, an unexpected and very strong snowstorm changed everything.

As usual, the people of the neighborhood headed off in their cars for work that morning. Their dogs were fed and left outside to enjoy the crisp fall air and bright sunshine.

Around noon, the snow began to fall… and fall… and fall. By 5 p.m. when work was finished, there was over a foot of snow on the ground.

Because it was October, the street crews had not been hired yet and the snowplow trucks weren't ready. No one had changed their tires to winter tires and they couldn't gain traction because of the deep snow. The people were stuck downtown!

Back in the neighborhood, the dogs had been enjoying the sudden change of weather. They were running and sliding and having a great time playing in the snow.

But then, it started to get dark and their stomachs began to rumble. "Hey, have you seen the people?" they shouted over their fences. And the answer was always, "No, they're not here."

Lucy had also been enjoying the afternoon. It was her first time ever seeing snow. She marveled as the light snowflakes melted when they landed on her warm nose.

Once the sun set, she too wondered where her family could be. But being an industrious former street dog, she'd hidden food in several spots in her backyard earlier that summer. She simply dug down into the snow and found a hidden tasty stash of kibble.

As she ate, she heard the other dogs barking at each other. She still couldn't understand what they were saying but she could tell by the tone of their barks they were worried about something. Lucy poked her head over the fence and asked her next-door neighbor, "¿Qué está pasando?", meaning "What's happening?" He, of course, didn't understand her, and she couldn't follow his answer.

Dogs are good problem solvers and they love having a task to complete. This was important, so instead of giving up or being frustrated, they both tilted their heads to the side, sniffed the air, and figured out a way to communicate.

¡Perros preocupados!

Her neighbor began pushing snow around with his nose and making gestures with his paws. Soon, Lucy realized the reason she had to find her own dinner was the same reason the others were barking. The neighborhood was filled with worried and hungry dogs!

Lucy knew just what to do. First, she dug up all her food stashes. Then, she placed the kibble in a sledding saucer, which was stored on the side of the house, and pushed it over to the gate. She'd learned how to nudge the latch with her nose to let herself out when she first arrived. This helped her feel less trapped in her fenced yard.

She started with her neighbor. Again, she nudged the latch with her nose and let herself into his backyard. Once he'd been fed, they set off together to help the other dogs.

With wagging tails, they went from house to house and shared Lucy's food with the other dogs.

Each time a new dog was fed, they would join the pack and its exciting task. Just like a member of the caravan from Panama, Lucy was part of a group who was trying to make their situation better. And for the first time in a long time, she felt happy.

It took about an hour but eventually, all the dogs were fed. Just then, lights began to appear in the houses. The roads had been cleared and the people were back home safe!

The people were surprised to see their dogs outside their backyards but what they found even more surprising was that they were all happily surrounding the new dog they had always avoided. They were clearly celebrating Lucy, but why?

The reason was soon learned. Lucy's adoptive family found all the holes she had dug in the snow around their house. They explained to everyone that Lucy must have stored her food in their backyard and used her hidden stash to feed the hungry dogs.

The dogs realized they were wrong about Lucy. What was different about her made her awesome. Her difficult early years in Panama had prepared her for life's uncertainties. She couldn't express herself clearly but she would learn.

The neighborhood dogs wanted to learn too. What did the unusual sounds Lucy made mean? Could she teach them to think ahead and plan for a snowy day?

Lucy had helped them, so they collectively decided to help her. They'd be more patient with her and teach her how things worked in the neighborhood and in the US.

Lucy still had tough days when she missed Panama. Learning a new language and culture is hard work but she didn't have to do it alone. She now had new friends and a welcoming community to support her. She was finally home.

Very loosely based on the life and times of the real Lucy—a sassy and adventurous Panamanian Chica.

Thank you to everyone who has shown enthusiasm for this book. Without your excitement and support, I'm not sure if I would have followed through and made this idea real. Political gamesmanship has led to a crisis of rejected and misunderstood masses the world over. Using the filter of a dog seeking belly rubs and an indoor bed, I hope to inject some empathy into the conversation. We all seek a better life for ourselves and our loved ones. Today's kids are tomorrow's voters, so here's hoping they remember our heroine, Lucy, when they are of age to change the world.

Thank you to Tereza Racekova for editing the manuscript and the myriad of other details she helped me with. As a first-time writer, I needed her expert eye and thoughtful refinement.

The Faune typeface used in this document was created by Alice Savoie in the context of a commission by the Centre National des Arts Plastiques in partnership with the Groupe Imprimerie Nationale.

Thank you for buying and reading this book. Please share this story with your friends and family.

www.ingramcontent.com/pod-product-compliance
Lightning Source LLC
Chambersburg PA
CBHW041441010526
44118CB00003B/148